Bert's Shirt

by Natalie Lambert
illustrated by Margeaux Lucas

Practice Decodable 41

I0806507

McGraw Hill Education

Bothell, WA • Chicago, IL • Columbus, OH • New York, NY

MHEonline.com

Send all inquiries to:
McGraw-Hill Education
8787 Orion Place
Columbus, OH 43240

ISBN: 978-0-02-135424-5
MHID: 0-02-135424-3

Printed in the United States of America.

7 8 9 CTM 23

Bert wore a fresh shirt.

Will Bert get dirt on it?

Bert did a lot.

First, Bert stirred eggs.

Next, Bert helped a girl.
Bert helped her spread jam.

Third, Bert filled small cups.
Last, Bert cut bread.

Did Bert get dirt on his shirt?

Dirt did get on Bert's shirt.
Lots of spots are on Bert's shirt.